Tell Me the Truth About Love

About Love

Tell Me the Truth About Love

TEN POEMS BY

W. H. Auden

VINTAGE BOOKS

A Division of Random House, Inc.

New York

A Vintage Original, May 1994
FIRST EDITION

ISBN 0-679-75782-1

Manufactured in the United States of America

10 9 8 7 6

Contents

O Tell Me the Truth About Love

Some say that love's a little boy,
          And some say it's a bird,
Some say it makes the world go round,
          And some say that's absurd,
And when I asked the man next-door,
          Who looked as if he knew,
His wife got very cross indeed,
          And said it wouldn't do.

Does it look like a pair of pyjamas,
　　Or the ham in a temperance hotel?
Does its odour remind one of llamas,
　　Or has it a comforting smell?
Is it prickly to touch as a hedge is,
　　Or soft as eiderdown fluff?
Is it sharp or quite smooth at the edges?
　　O tell me the truth about love.

Our history books refer to it
　　　　In cryptic little notes,
It's quite a common topic on
　　　　The Transatlantic boats;
I've found the subject mentioned in
　　　　Accounts of suicides,
And even seen it scribbled on
　　　　The backs of railway-guides.

Does it howl like a hungry Alsatian,
　　Or boom like a military band?
Could one give a first-rate imitation
　　On a saw or a Steinway Grand?
Is its singing at parties a riot?
　　Does it only like Classical stuff?
Will it stop when one wants to be quiet?
　　O tell me the truth about love.

I looked inside the summer-house;
　　　　It wasn't ever there:
I tried the Thames at Maidenhead,
　　　　And Brighton's bracing air.
I don't know what the blackbird sang,
　　　　Or what the tulip said;
But it wasn't in the chicken-run,
　　　　Or underneath the bed.

Can it pull extraordinary faces?
    Is it usually sick on a swing?
Does it spend all its time at the races,
    Or fiddling with pieces of string?
Has it views of its own about money?
    Does it think Patriotism enough?
Are its stories vulgar but funny?
    O tell me the truth about love.

When it comes, will it come without warning
    Just as I'm picking my nose?
Will it knock on my door in the morning,
    Or tread in the bus on my toes?
Will it come like a change in the weather?
    Will its greeting be courteous or rough?
Will it alter my life altogether?
    O tell me the truth about love.

Song

Fish in the unruffled lakes
Their swarming colours wear,
Swans in the winter air
A white perfection have,
And the great lion walks
Through his innocent grove;
Lion, fish and swan
Act, and are gone
Upon Time's toppling wave.

We, till shadowed days are done,
We must weep and sing
Duty's conscious wrong,
The Devil in the clock,
The goodness carefully worn
For atonement or for luck;
We must lose our loves,
On each beast and bird that moves
Turn an envious look.

Sighs for folly done and said
Twist our narrow days,
But I must bless, I must praise
That you, my swan, who have
All gifts that to the swan
Impulsive Nature gave,
The majesty and pride,
Last night should add
Your voluntary love.

Underneath an Abject Willow

Underneath an abject willow,
   Lover, sulk no more:
Act from thought should quickly follow.
   What is thinking for?
Your unique and moping station
   Proves you cold;
   Stand up and fold
Your map of desolation.

Bells that toll across the meadows
    From the sombre spire
Toll for these unloving shadows
    Love does not require.
All that lives may love; why longer
    Bow to loss
    With arms across?
Strike and you shall conquer.

Geese in flocks above you flying,
    Their direction know,
Icy brooks beneath you flowing,
    To their ocean go.
Dark and dull is your distraction:
    Walk then, come,
    No longer numb
Into your satisfaction.

Calypso

Driver drive faster and make a good rún
Down the Springfield Line únder the shining sún.

Flý like an aéroplane, dón't pull up shórt
Till you bráke for Grand Céntral Státion, New Yórk.

For thére in the míddle of thát waiting-háll
Should be stánding the óne that Í love best of áll.

If he's nót there to méet me when Í get to tówn,
I'll stánd on the síde-walk with téars rolling dówn.

For hé is the óne that I lóve to look ón,
The ácme of kíndness and pérfectión.

He présses my hánd and he sáys he loves mé,
Which I fínd an admiráble pecúliaritý.

The wóods are bright gréen on both sídes of the líne;
The trées have their lóves though they're different from míne.

But the póor fat old bánker in the sún-parlor cár
Has nó one to lóve him excépt his cigár.

If Í were the Héad of the Chúrch or the Státe,
I'd pówder my nóse and just téll them to wáit.

For lóve's more impórtant and pówerful thán
Éven a príest or a póliticián.

As I Walked Out One Evening

As I walked out one evening,
   Walking down Bristol Street,
The crowds upon the pavement
   Were fields of harvest wheat.

And down by the brimming river
   I heard a lover sing
Under an arch of the railway:
   "Love has no ending.

"I'll love you, dear, I'll love you
    Till China and Africa meet,
  And the river jumps over the mountain
    And the salmon sing in the street,

"I'll love you till the ocean
    Is folded and hung up to dry
  And the seven stars go squawking
    Like geese about the sky.

"The years shall run like rabbits,
    For in my arms I hold
  The Flower of the Ages,
    And the first love of the world."

But all the clocks in the city
    Began to whirr and chime:
"O let not Time deceive you,
    You cannot conquer Time.

"In the burrows of the Nightmare
  Where Justice naked is,
 Time watches from the shadow
  And coughs when you would kiss.

"In headaches and in worry
  Vaguely life leaks away,
 And Time will have his fancy
  To-morrow or to-day.

"Into many a green valley
  Drifts the appalling snow;
 Time breaks the threaded dances
  And the diver's brilliant bow.

"O plunge your hands in water,
  Plunge them in up to the wrist;
 Stare, stare in the basin
  And wonder what you've missed.

"The glacier knocks in the cupboard,
    The desert sighs in the bed,
And the crack in the tea-cup opens
    A lane to the land of the dead.

"Where the beggars raffle the banknotes
    And the Giant is enchanting to Jack,
And the Lily-white Boy is a Roarer,
    And Jill goes down on her back.

"O look, look in the mirror,
    O look in your distress;
Life remains a blessing
    Although you cannot bless.

"O stand, stand at the window
    As the tears scald and start;
You shall love your crooked neighbour
    With your crooked heart."

It was late, late in the evening,
    The lovers they were gone;
The clocks had ceased their chiming,
    And the deep river ran on.

Lullaby

Lay your sleeping head, my love,
Human on my faithless arm;
Time and fevers burn away
Individual beauty from
Thoughtful children, and the grave
Proves the child ephemeral:
But in my arms till break of day
Let the living creature lie,
Mortal, guilty, but to me
The entirely beautiful.

Soul and body have no bounds:
To lovers as they lie upon
Her tolerant enchanted slope
In their ordinary swoon,
Grave the vision Venus sends
Of supernatural sympathy,
Universal love and hope;
While an abstract insight wakes
Among the glaciers and the rocks
The hermit's carnal ecstasy.

Certainty, fidelity
On the stroke of midnight pass
Like vibrations of a bell
And fashionable madmen raise
Their pedantic boring cry:
Every farthing of the cost,
All the dreaded cards foretell,
Shall be paid, but from this night
Not a whisper, not a thought,
Not a kiss nor look be lost.

Beauty, midnight, vision dies:
Let the winds of dawn that blow
Softly round your dreaming head
Such a day of welcome show
Eye and knocking heart may bless,
Find our mortal world enough;
Noons of dryness find you fed
By the involuntary powers,
Nights of insult let you pass
Watched by every human love.

At Last
the Secret Is Out

At last the secret is out,
        as it always must come in the end,
The delicious story is ripe
        to tell to the intimate friend;
Over the tea-cups and in the square
        the tongue has its desire;
Still waters run deep, my dear,
        there's never smoke without fire.

Behind the corpse in the reservoir,
        behind the ghost on the links,
Behind the lady who dances
        and the man who madly drinks,
Under the look of fatigue,
        the attack of migraine and the sigh
There is always another story,
        there is more than meets the eye.

For the clear voice suddenly singing,
        high up in the convent wall,
The scent of the elder bushes,
        the sporting prints in the hall,
The croquet matches in summer,
        the handshake, the cough, the kiss,
There is always a wicked secret,
        a private reason for this.

O What Is That Sound

O what is that sound which so thrills the ear
  Down in the valley drumming, drumming?
Only the scarlet soldiers, dear,
  The soldiers coming.

O what is that light I see flashing so clear
  Over the distance brightly, brightly?
Only the sun on their weapons, dear,
  As they step lightly.

O what are they doing with all that gear,
  What are they doing this morning, this morning?
Only their usual manoeuvres, dear,
  Or perhaps a warning.

O why have they left the road down there,
  Why are they suddenly wheeling, wheeling?
Perhaps a change in their orders, dear.
  Why are you kneeling?

O haven't they stopped for the doctor's care,
  Haven't they reined their horses, their horses?
Why, they are none of them wounded, dear,
  None of these forces.

O is it the parson they want, with white hair,
  Is it the parson, is it, is it?
No, they are passing his gateway, dear,
  Without a visit.

O it must be the farmer who lives so near.

   It must be the farmer so cunning, so cunning?

They have passed the farmyard already, dear,

   And now they are running.

O where are you going? Stay with me here!

   Were the vows you swore deceiving, deceiving?

No, I promised to love you, dear,

   But I must be leaving.

O it's broken the lock and splintered the door,

   O it's the gate where they're turning, turning;

Their boots are heavy on the floor

   And their eyes are burning.

Johnny

O the valley in the summer where I and my John
Beside the deep river would walk on and on
While the flowers at our feet and the birds up above
Argued so sweetly on reciprocal love,
And I leaned on his shoulder; "O Johnny, let's play":
But he frowned like thunder and he went away.

O that Friday near Christmas as I well recall
When we went to the Charity Matinee Ball,
The floor was so smooth and the band was so loud
And Johnny so handsome I felt so proud;
"Squeeze me tighter, dear Johnny, let's dance till it's day":
But he frowned like thunder and he went away.

Shall I ever forget at the Grand Opera
When music poured out of each wonderful star?
Diamonds and pearls they hung dazzling down
Over each silver or golden silk gown;
"O John I'm in heaven," I whispered to say:
But he frowned like thunder and he went away.

O but he was as fair as a garden in flower,
As slender and tall as the great Eiffel Tower,
When the waltz throbbed out on the long promenade
O his eyes and his smile they went straight to my heart;
"O marry me, Johnny, I'll love and obey":
But he frowned like thunder and he went away.

O last night I dreamed of you, Johnny, my lover,
You'd the sun on one arm and the moon on the other,
The sea it was blue and the grass it was green,
Every star rattled a round tambourine;
Ten thousand miles deep in a pit there I lay:
But you frowned like thunder and you went away.

Funeral Blues

Stop all the clocks, cut off the telephone,
Prevent the dog from barking with a juicy bone,
Silence the pianos and with muffled drum
Bring out the coffin, let the mourners come.

Let aeroplanes circle moaning overhead
Scribbling on the sky the message He Is Dead,
Put crêpe bows round the white necks of the public doves,
Let the traffic policemen wear black cotton gloves.

He was my North, my South, my East and West,
My working week and my Sunday rest,
My noon, my midnight, my talk, my song;
I thought that love would last for ever: I was wrong.

The stars are not wanted now: put out every one;
Pack up the moon and dismantle the sun;
Pour away the ocean and sweep up the wood;
For nothing now can ever come to any good.

About the Author

WYSTAN HUGH AUDEN was born in York, England, on February 21, 1907. His father was a professor of public health and his mother a nurse. After studying at Oxford, he lived for a year in a Berlin slum, then returned to England, where he worked as a schoolmaster from 1930 through 1935. After 1935 he made his living as a free-lance writer, working first in a documentary film unit, then writing travel books about Iceland and China. He wrote the poems in this collection between 1932 and 1939. Many of them were written to be set to music by Benjamin Britten and sung by the soprano Hedli Anderson; an early version of "Funeral Blues" was set by Britten for *The Ascent of F6,* one of three plays Auden wrote with Christopher Isherwood. Auden moved to New York in 1939, and became an American citizen in 1946. From 1941 through 1945 he taught at American colleges, and then again made his living as a free-lance writer. From 1948 until the end of his life he spent his summers in Europe, first in Italy, then, after 1958, in Austria. In 1972 he left his winter home in New York to return to Oxford, and died in Vienna on September 29, 1973. All the poems in this collection also appear in his *Collected Poems* (Vintage International).

EDWARD MENDELSON, the compiler of this volume, is the literary executor of the Estate of W. H. Auden.